MW00605249

IMAGES
of America

DRACUT

Workers at the Beaver Brook Mill, Navy Yard, Dracut.

IMAGES
of America

DRACUT

John Pendergast

ARCADIA
PUBLISHING

Published by Arcadia Publishing
Charleston, South Carolina

Library of Congress Catalog Card Number: 2008939728

For all general information contact Arcadia Publishing at:
Telephone 843-853-2070
Fax 843-853-0044
E-mail sales@arcadiapublishing.com
For customer service and orders:
Toll-Free 1-888-313-2665

Visit us on the Internet at www.arcadiapublishing.com

On the Cover: The employees of the Navy Yard Mills, Pleasant Street, Dracut, 1880s.

Contents

Preface

I was born in Centralville, on Bridge Street, in Lowell, but I have always considered Dracut to be my home, although I have twice been reminded by prominent old Dracuteers that I was "not from Dracut; not from Dracut at all." I spent as much of my childhood on Pleasant Street where my grandfather lived and in the Navy Yard as I did on the North Common (we moved from Bridge Street to the Acre when I was about three months old). In 1951, when I was twelve, my mother, who was born in Dracut and never lost her deep connections with the town, took me on a bus tour to many of the old Dracut houses. I remember seeing many, like the Durkee House (1652) with musket ball holes still in its walls, that are now long gone. It was her deep affection for the town that sparked my interest. I was still in Keith Academy when we moved to Dracut and I drove into the city for the last year. After graduating from Lowell Teachers College, I taught junior high school at the Greenmont Avenue School, where years earlier when it was still the high school, I saw my Uncle Tom do his famous Al Jolson act at the annual minstrel show. Inside there's a photograph of the first graduating class from that school. I was elected first president of the Dracut Junior Chamber of Commerce; later I followed my younger brother Pat as president of the Dracut Historical Society. My uncle Jack, who was Dracut's postmaster for a long while, as well as a marathon runner and World War II naval hero, and I would drive around on Christmas Eve delivering gifts to kids of local families with financial problems. He would drive the truck and I, dressed as Santa, would go into the houses to looks of amazement with bags of donated gifts. I imposed my opinions of ancient history and literature on Dracut adolescents for several years, held bean suppers in the Grange Hall with the Jaycees, and attended innumerable Dracut weddings, christenings, graduations, and funerals.

It wasn't until I left to go to Ireland for a few years that I developed a greater understanding and deeper affection for Dracut. To view the town from 3,500 miles away; to be walking to my Dublin apartment the mile or two from the National Library, alone, often in the Irish rain, with the objectivity that comes with distance, I envisioned Dracut as a secure, tranquil, verdant haven with a sprawling American comfortableness and native confidence which stemmed back to its earliest days when it was still called *Augumtoocooke*, "The Wilderness North of the River." It represented for me a typical New England town with a brilliant but almost forgotten past. It was more than that—as well as the Yankee tradition, there were the unusually early ethnic arrivals. Dracut has an old population of Irish, Greeks, Poles, and French-Canadians. Michael Collins founded the Collinsville Mills and hired many Irish and Irish-Americans when the "No Irish Need Apply" signs were common in many other places. There was once a Jewish section of town at Long Pond. The earliest French-Canadians to arrive were refugees from British cruelty. Black families owned land in Kenwood before the Revolution. These early arrivals set the town off from most New England villages. When I taught junior high school in Dublin, almost all of the students were Irish, had Irish names, gestures, expressions, and other characteristics. I recalled my students in Dracut—names like DiVicenzi, Malliaros, Hudzik, O'Toole, Richardson, Litchfield, Stott, Frawley, Shanley, Knox, Daigle, Swiniarski, Tsouprakakis, Therriault—the list goes on far further.

Introduction

Dracut was founded February 26, 1701—or was it 1702. Until 1752, England and her colonies clung to the old style of dating in which February was the last month of the year and March 1 was New Years' Day. Most everywhere else in the western world that particular February was in 1702. However, the Dracut town seal reads 1701, and the tricentennial celebrations will surely reflect that year.

We will never know when the first human walked on the soil that is now Dracut, but tools imply a Late Paleolithic occupation, perhaps as early as ten or eleven thousand years ago. Tools that date before this time are rarely found anywhere in New England, so the initial inhabitants may have arrived even earlier. They were nomadic, carnivorous (so the tools tell us), and probably didn't organize into large tribal groups with names until about three thousand years ago (some anthropologists think even more recently). Here they were called Pawtuckets; they were part of a larger group called Pennacook in the early histories, but today they are known by social scientists as the Western Abnaki (for linguistic reasons). Europeans were here earlier, but in 1607, Samuel de Champlain was the first European recorded to sail up the Merrimac. It is not known if Champlain came up as far as Dracut. John Smith, of Pocahontas fame, more likely did in 1611. The Pennacook nation ranged from about ten miles south of the Merrimac north to the St. Lawrence River. They lived along the river basin. The land between the Merrimac basin and the Connecticut basin, which was inhabited by the Mohawk, the enemy, was no-man's-land. The Pennacook had developed horticulture by the time the Europeans had arrived, but not all of the other New England groups had. The Tarrantine from Maine, among other hostile groups, would come down and murder local natives in order to raid their storage pits.

In 1617, or thereabouts, 85 percent of the local native population succumbed to European disease, to which they had no immunities (these are far more horrific statistics than those of the Black Plague, which only killed one-third of Northwestern Europe in 1348–50). The last ruler of all these Pennacook, whose domain stretched far north to Canada, chose to live along the river in Dracut. His name was Passaconaway, "The Child of the Bear." In 1660, in front of the largest Pennacook gathering ever known, at the Pawtucket Falls he told his people not to fight against the White Man, ". . . whose Gods are more powerful than ours." He then resigned his position to his son Wannalancit and disappeared into the wilderness. By 1680, there were no more Pawtucket in Dracut.

Dracut's first landowner was John Webb, who had an alias (Evered). He ultimately fled back to Boston after being involved in a dark scandal. He was killed when ropes from a harpoon he plunged into a whale in Boston Harbor wrapped around his body. The whale sounded and he was drawn into the water. His wife sold his lands in Dracut to the first resident, Edward Coburn. The strong theory is that Dracut was named after Webb's English birthplace, Draycott-Foliat in Wiltshire, but there are other suggestions postulated. In any case, there is no other place called Dracut—anywhere.

In 1671, there were six taxpayers: Samuel Varnum and Edward Coburn and his four sons. In 1675, during King Philip's War, two of Samuel Varnum's sons were killed by Indian musket balls as they crossed the river at a place just below the Rourke Bridge. These are the only two victims of warfare ever killed within Dracut boundaries in recorded history.

The town did not exhibit pacifism nor passivity however. A higher percentage of the male population from Dracut went to fight in the Revolutionary War than from any other community in the thirteen colonies. One of them, Enoch Frye, was only twelve years old. Dracut has produced an unusual number of nationally important military, political, and business leaders. Marquis de Lafayette came to visit an old aristocratic friend in Dracut after the Revolution. The first spool of thread in the Western Hemisphere was wound in Dracut. The first summer stock theater originated at Lakeview Park. The very sound of the name of the town is pleasing and as harmonious as the place it represents. It has always meant home.

One

Some of the People

Miss Mabel L. Wilcox's class at the New Boston School on Hildreth Street, 1904–1905. Miss Wilcox married Arthur W. Colburn on September 20, 1905.

The Curtis Farm on Broadway Road facing Fox Avenue, *c.* 1880. Town records read, "on Oct. 29, 1756, the French family, being nine in number came to Dracutt and abode at the house of Ephraim Curtis. . ." A few of the many Arcadian refugees, taken by force from their Nova Scotia farms and dispersed along the English colonial Atlantic coast, were taken in and virtually saved from starvation by Dracut families. Landerie or Landry was one of the family names. After several years of residency, money was collected among residents to defray some passages to "Quebck" *[sic]*— many stayed.

Classes at the East Dracut Church, 1880s.

The happy couple. Arthur and Mabel (Wilcox) Colburn leave for their wedding trip to the White Mountains, September 29, 1905. Arthur Colburn owned the first automobile in Dracut. The Colburns arrived in Dracut in the 1660s.

Daniel Cameron, a farmer and milk dealer on Mammoth Road near Mill Street in the 1890s. Here, he sits on his porch with his brother and an unidentified gentleman.

Dracut Center Church picnic, June 26, 1881. The setting is actually North Billerica, but the participants are Dracut people. September 6 of this year was known for years later as the "Yellow Day." Trees, grass, buildings, and people all took on a yellow hue. It was necessary to use artificial light in the middle of the day. By noon the darkness had increased enough to frighten the superstitious. At 3:30 pm, all was well again. No satisfactory explanation was ever given. On May 19, 1790, a similar phenomenon occurred. Cocks crowed all day; the sky was red, yellow, and brown. All things appeared to be tinged with yellow, and cows came from the pastures at noon to be milked.

Sisters in law, 1895. Seated is Miss Lucinda Mansur, daughter of Daniel Mansur. Mrs. Joshua Francis (Hitchock) Mansur, wife of Daniel's son William, stands beside her. The photograph was taken outside the family homestead, which was purchased by Joshua from other family members in 1862. Lucinda died in 1906.

Members of the Yap family in the early 1870s on the farm at Marsh Hill.

Parker Avenue School, 1890s. The teacher is Miss Brown. A female teacher in Dracut could expect to earn about two dollars per week including board. This building burned in 1923.

The Curtis family with bicycles, Broadway Road, *c.* 1880.

Calvin Richardson and John Peabody. The two men sit among the foliage and bunting in the Old Yellow Meeting House decorated for the 200th anniversary of the founding of Dracut. The photograph is dated June 12, 1901.

Calvin Coolidge, who came to Hovey Square in the mid- to late 1920s. The old Hovey house, no longer extant, is in the background; it was a tavern in the late 1700s.

Thomas Hovey purchased land here before the Revolution and built the tavern. The military training grounds were adjacent and Bradley's Ferry across the Merrimac—leading up Bridge Street to the northern towns—passed its doors. According to Silas Coburn, "It must have been a favorite place for citizens to meet and discuss the situation when news came of the oppressive acts of the British Ministry . . . lady passengers were served hot tea passed from the windows without alighting from the coach." John Varnum records in his journal, "29 May 1777. In the forenoon attended on training &c. No Rhum, flip nor Cyder to be had at ye Tavern, the first training of that kind ever heard of in Dracut."

A closer view of Coolidge in Hovey Square.

An early photograph of George Englesby's family home on School Street, c. 1875. George Englesby was a well-known, personable local educator and administrator of the 1940s to the '60s. The Englesby Junior High School was named for him. His father was a day watchman at the Navy Yard Mills.

Lillian and Leo Moore, c. 1936. This couple lived at the bottom of Hovey Square Hill at 211 Pleasant Street; Leo was present at the Liberation of Paris in 1945, and Lillian was a news reporter and a well-known personality who lived all of her life in Dracut.

The Keefe family. Marietta and Ricky Keefe and son Thomas celebrate his 4th of July birthday party, c. 1932. Marietta and Ricky were well-known dancers. Ricky was a champion swimmer, motorman for the Eastern Massachusetts Bus Company, and more than a dabbler in army surplus sales. In the years following World War II, the cellar of his 188 Pleasant Street house was filled with woolen stockings, combat boots, gloves, pants, shirts, belts, etc. Many Dracut residents wore khaki and marine green in those years.

Mr. and Mrs. Henry LaMountain, who lived at 39 Pleasant Street close to the Navy Yard Mills. Mr. LaMountain wears his Civil War veteran's medal. He was a male nurse, *c.* 1905.

Elizabeth Collier Stickney, wife of Asa Stickney. Elizabeth was the daughter of Alexander Collier of 195 Pleasant Street.

George Stevens. Born in Lowell, Stevens moved to Dracut at age six. He traveled to the far west and worked for the Oregon Railroad and Steamship Company, but returned while still a young man. He was Dracut's postman at the end of the last century. Among his other titles, he was justice of the peace, selectman, chief of police, and deputy sheriff. He was the first president of the Dracut Historical Society in 1935.

Moise Daigle and family sitting in the new trap. Louis Daigle, his father, purchased the Old Curtis Farm on Broadway and Fox Avenue (seen in earlier photographs). He was a blacksmith and lived at this address with his large family. This same house served as a refuge for French-Canadian families in 1756 was later owned by a French-Canadian family.

Rear Admiral Joseph G. Eaton with his daughter Isabelle and his first wife, Annie (Varnum) Eaton. During the Spanish American War, Admiral Eaton commanded the ammunition ship *Resolute* and the battleship *Massachusetts*, among others. He received a Medal of Honor for his part in the Battle of Santiago during the Spanish-American War. There were two Medal of Honor recipients from Dracut during this conflict. Eaton died in 1913.

Another portrait of Admiral Eaton. He is buried in the Oakland Cemetery.

A formal occasion, evidenced by the proliferation of black bow ties at the Hillside Church on Pleasant Street. The church was torn down about twenty years ago. Included in this c. 1940 photograph are Larry Litchfield, Clarence Nichols, Fred Eldridge, Rev. Clyde Kimball, John Crane, Robert Horton, Harold Mockery, James Shanks, Jerry Boulton, Tommy Inch, Albert Eldridge, Tom Clarke, Jack Hickey, Ed Dundle, George Gunther, Bob Crane, Bill Kearns, Robert Tryon, Bill Drendle, and Fred Birchenaugh.

Mrs. Martha Little Davidson. Mrs. Davidson spooled the first spool of cotton thread ever wound in the Western Hemisphere. She was sent to Paisley, Scotland, the world center of thread manufacture, and then to Liverpool to learn the process. She returned to Dracut and began to operate her spindle in June of 1844.

View from the hangars at Richardson's Airport on Lakeview Avenue in the late 1940s. This is presently the site of the police station and junior high school.

The family of Clemens and Minnie Gunther at the turn of the century. The Gunthers lived at 28 Swain Street The descendants of this family saw the bright future possible in automobile repair and maintenance, and they still work at this profession in town.

The Florence Club, an athletic organization centered about the Navy Yard.

A family of Foxes, *c.* 1905. Pictured are, from left to right: (front row) D. Stedman Fox (father), Albert Fox (milk dealer), and Maria Fox (mother); (back row) Harry Fox (town clerk) stands with his sister, Jennie, (mother of Pauline Varnum, a member of Dracut's first high school faculty).

Funeral of firefighter John Dillon, August, 31, 1934. Dillon was killed in a fire truck accident while on duty. The bearers were: James Dillon (brother), Ernest Patterson (Collinsville district), Captain John McPherson, Lieutenant Wilfred Langlois, Larrie Lindfors, and Captain Gustave Roth.

Confirmation class at Saint Mary's Church, c. 1930. On the left is John F. Kiernan, Collinsville's postmaster, and Father Landigan (next to the bishop).

St. Mary of the Assumption Church on Lakeview Avenue before renovations.

St. Theresa's Church on Lakeview Avenue. The church burned down on January 21, 1938.

St. Theresa's—rebuilt, enlarged, and safer. This postcard dates to the mid-1950s.

(Left) Izella Colburn, one of the many members of the Colburn/Coburn family to live in Dracut. Her ancestor, Edward Colburn, was the first person to cross the Merrimac River in the 1650s from the Chelmsford side to settle in what later became Dracut. (Right) Walter G. Hall, son of Gayton Hall. He held several town offices including town clerk in 1895.

(Left) John Sparks. When John Sparks returned from the Great War, he became a druggist at 716 Lakeview Avenue, which was located across from Brunet's Lunch Cafe, now the Cameo Diner. (Right) G.P. Varnum, who descended from the second family to settle in Dracut. His family claims many other illustrious descendants, including military leaders, scholars, and pioneer abolitionists.

Joseph Parker Varnum, also descended from the Varnums of Dracut. His farm was on Varnum Avenue, the second oldest road in town, on land which had been in his family since 1664. Dracut's earliest roads were along or heading toward the river, such as Ferry Lane, the first road on the northern side of the river. Only when population and livestock needed more acreage did the roads begin to penetrate the wilderness north of the river.

Joseph Bradley Varnum. Varnum was born, lived, and died in Dracut on the farm left to him by his father on the corner of Methuen Street and Parker Avenue (burned in 1872). He was Dracut's captain of minutemen and fought at the battle of Lexington. He was in the Massachusetts State Legislature from 1781 to 1785. Varnum was also Speaker of the House (1807–1811), and a senator in the U.S. Congress (1811–1817).

Raymond Archibald Willette making a delivery. He is in one of the Beaver Brook Farm wagons owned by farmer Justus C. Richardson, who lived at the family farm at 770 Mammoth Road. Mr. Richardson donated the land for Dracut High School. The Richardsons arrived in Dracut in 1712.

Another photograph of Ray, this time in 1915 on a vehicle featuring a different kind of horsepower.

Brookside Social and Athletic Club, Collinsville, no date.

Two

Some of Their Places

The Abbot House, just north of Hovey Square on Hildreth Street, built about 1757. In front is Lucella Abbot Willoughby (1833–1916), the last Abbot to reside in the house. This house was on the stagecoach road from Concord, NH, to Boston. Five men from the Abbot family in Dracut fought in the Revolutionary War.

The Captain Stephen Russell House, built about 1695 and still at 533 Pleasant Street. Captain Russell led a company of Dracut militiamen which marched to join the battle of Lexington on April 19, 1775.

Dracut Grange Hall on Bridge Street, next to the Old Yellow Meeting House, from a postcard made about six years after it was built in 1907. Functions are still held at the hall.

The Stephens-Boulton store on Pleasant and Sladen Streets. There has been a store at this location for over 150 years. It is presently a tuxedo rental shop.

The Dracut Center School. Built on Arlington Street in 1883, the school was remodeled as town offices in 1898. The building, though unrecognizable in this picture, still houses the town offices.

The Ezechial Hale house. This home was moved from the corner of Lakeview and Pleasant Streets to Lakeview Avenue, next door to the appliance store on the corner. Ezechial Hale ran a woolen mill just below the dam on Pleasant Street in the 1760s. The house was razed early in this century.

The Lillian Moore house at 265 Pleasant Street. It was moved from its original location on Greenmount Avenue by Samuel Newall Harrison in the nineteenth century. It predates the Revolutionary War and has (had?) a secret stairway from a second floor bedroom down to an underground passage.

Members of the Dracut High School Sophomore Class of 1938, some of whom have been painstakingly identified: (front row) 2. Dorothy Gunther, 4. Catherine Demitropoulos, 5. Alice Fuller, 6. Gladys Harne, 7. Connie Neofotistos, 8. Alice Juscyak, 9. Stephanie Ras, 10. Laura Hall, 11. Helen Sterns, 12. Eileen Sturtevant, 15. Stella Tymula, 17. Ann Michalczyk, and 18. Virginia Robinson; (second row) 2. Doris Allen, 3. Annie Neofotistos, 6. Josephine Wasylak, 8. Mary Cauney, 9, Marjorie Gunther, 11. Barbara Doris, 12. Stasia Christynia, and 14. Anna Christynia; (third row) 1. Jennie Kinder, 3. Flora Shanks, and 5. Stella Bletsis; (fourth row) 1. William Socorelis, 2. Allen Fox, 4. Leo Alexakos, 5. Stanley Lachut, 6. John King, 8. Edward Normandin, 9. Alfred Grondine, and 10. Wallace Sheppard; (fifth row) 1. Kenneth Maddocks, 3. Dexter Dutney, 8. Albert Vermette, and 10. Frank Merrill; (sixth row) 2. Howard Liddy, 3. Earl Frappier, 4. Willis Laskey, 6. Telemachus Demoulas, 8. Robert Monahan, and 9. Raymond Peters.

The same class as on the previous page, but as seventh graders in 1935.

The only known photograph of the East Dracut School, undated.

Home built by Zachariah Goodhue Jr. in 1779. He constructed this house when he married Mrs. Toothaker of Billerica. It was on the corner of Pleasant and Sladen Streets. The Goodhue School was built on the site of the barn and the house itself was torn down to enlarge the school grounds.

Residence of Lowell W. Colburn. This stone house still stands on Colburn Avenue.

Homestead of Captain Peter Colburn. Colburn led a company of Dracut minutemen to Lexington. He also brought them to Bunker Hill two months later. His father built the house which was on Mammoth Road just north of Passaconaway Drive. Believed to date from about 1670, the home burned in 1930.

Caretaker's house at Lakeview Park, 1900. Frank Dunlap of Tyngsborough was the first caretaker. Then came John Cody of Collinsville, then Matthew Urquhardt, whose daughter Polly was a well-known Collinsville businesswoman.

The Hildreth house. This abode stood in Hovey Square on the present-day site of Jimmy's Pizza. It was built in the late 1700s by Revolutionary War General William Hildreth. Two enormous fireplaces heated the ballroom which extended along the entire front of the second floor. From 1916 until the 1950s, the house served as a hospital. It burned in 1965.

Number 2 Pleasant Street. This little house still sits (with a few alterations) at 2 Pleasant Street.

The Dracut Town Offices, still in use in 1898, on Willard Street at Cheever Avenue.

The Broadway School, on the corner of Jones Avenue, built in 1900. It is now a residence.

Colburn Avenue, looking towards Pelham. This view is one of the oldest photographs in the Dracut Historical Society's collection. It was taken in the mid-1870s. On the back of the photograph is written, "Old Colburn farm on the left–later burned. Old homestead on the right was burned in 1875. Nannie's birthplace. Plenty of bittersweet grows here."

The first bridge across the Merrimac. Situated at about the site of the present-day Pawtucket Bridge, the first bridge was built in 1792 by Parker Varnum of Dracut. Bradley's Ferry, the only means of communication between Dracut and Chelmsford, was on the site before the bridge was built. It was constructed entirely of wood. It was destroyed in 1804, and another wasn't completed until October 23, 1823. It operated as a toll bridge until 1861. This very early photograph must be of the bridge of that period because the next structure was constructed completely of iron and finished in 1871. This one was the first to be named "Pawtucket Bridge" after the natives who lived along the shores at one time. "Pawtucket" means waterfall, being composed of the parts "*pau*," a loud noise, and "*tuck*," meaning place. Passaconaway's tepee was on the Dracut side of the river at this site 350 years ago; his son Wannalancit had a longhouse on the opposite shore.

The Phineas Street Bridge, which served as a shortcut from Lakeview Avenue to Riverside Street and Pawtucketville. This photograph dates from the late 1880s. The bridge has been replaced often and has been out of commission for many years. It is presently being reconstructed.

The Timothy Frye house at 225 Pleasant Street. Timothy and Hannah Frye were in Dracut as early as 1758. Their son Timothy was born in 1762; at age fourteen he fought in the Revolution. Fryes lived in this house until 1898. It was later owned by the Keefe and then the Panagiotakos families. It was torn down in the 1970s.

The Bouchard Development, 1947. This was the first large-scale housing development in Dracut. The large street cutting across the foreground is Lakeview Avenue.

Three

Recreation

A swimming party at Beaver Brook, *c*. 1928. Ricky Keefe is surrounded by fellow enthusiasts. His son, Jack, at age seven, later Dracut postmaster and saxophonist, stands by his side.

Two bicycles waiting at Richardson's Airport on Lakeview Avenue in the late 1940s.

Ricky Keefe testing the waters of Beaver Brook, February 1926. His brother, George, looks on.

Town dignitaries on parade, Memorial Day, c. 1960. On board are Charlie Grondine, Paul Merrill, Mike Blatus, and Leo Grondine. Grandfather George Grondine salutes the camera.

Kathleen and Phil Hammer. The couple poses for the camera at their Jack and Jill party held upstairs at the town hall in 1959.

Tony's at the Lake, 1947. Warren Hill imitates Bing Crosby, and Norman and Dick Gauthier are in the front seat of the car they built themselves. The girl's last name is Davis, but it's not Bette. Tony's, on Tyngsborough Road just before the town line, is presently called Debbie's.

The Black North Inn. Presently the Village Inn, this restaurant has been in operation for over half a century.

The Cafe Pompeii on Long Pond Road, which has had several names over the past few years. This postcard photograph was taken in the restaurant's heyday, c. 1945.

Old Folks Concert by Dracut Center Church Ladies Aid Society, Hillside Church, June 1927.

The picnic grounds at Belle Grove. This lovely area was owned by Alice "Belle" (nee Varnum) Isherwood. She modified her large estate along the Merrimac to accommodate a dance hall, ice house, picnic area, amusements, playing fields, and cottages. The grove was very popular in the decades between the wars. It was devastated by the 1936 flood.

The Water Wagon, Lakeview Park, 1921. Matthew Urquhardt is at the reins. Lakeview Park's fame as a resort dates back to the 1870s.

Lakeview Park, *c.* 1921. The park had a shooting gallery, pool parlor, and bowling alleys, as well as a roller coaster and carousel.

The "bobby horses." No depiction of Lakeview could be complete without a photograph of these horses, which were hand-carved in Germany and were valued at hundreds of thousands of dollars. Apartment buildings are now on the site.

Picnic grove at the corner of Stewart Street and Tyngsborough Road, 1899. The merry-go-round was just over the hill. There was a dance hall and restaurant at the end of the tracks which predated the Lakeview Ballroom.

Tyngsborough Road looking towards Stewart Street, 1899. Workmen in the distance are widening the road to extend the trolley tracks. A track switch was installed so that cars could pass each other in order to continue to Nashua.

Widening Tyngsborough Road, 1899. The bowling alley is in the right foreground and the carousel is visible in the distance.

Lake Mascuppic (Lakeview), looking from Tyngsborough Road towards Willowdale Avenue, 1900. The old stone boundary wall runs right into the water.

The *Mascuppic*, one of the many steamboats carrying passengers on the lake *c.* 1888.

The boat landing at Willowdale Park, built about 1860 by Jonathan Bowers.

Boats for rent at Lakeview. This photograph was taken by Robert Wescott, a professional photographer from Lowell, *c.* 1905.

A turn-of-the-century postcard depicting Willowdale Avenue along the lake.

Willowdale beach, 1900.

Landing for the steamer *Willowdale*, c. 1900.

Willowdale Station. The back of this postcard reads: "Willowdale Station, Lake Mascuppic, Dracut, Mass. Charles E. Delaney, Owner and Proprietor." No date is given.

The Willowdale Hotel, opened in 1861. This was later the site of Willowdale Spa and is now, like most of the old amusement areas, a residential neighborhood. The steamer *Kitty B* (on the far right) sank several yards offshore and is still visible when the water is low.

A close look at the steamer *Willowdale*, c. 1900. The tour, which cost 5¢, circled the entire lake.

A postcard sent from Miss Millicent Adams to her mother in Fall River, 1910. One can see that the trolley stopped right at the park entrance.

A closer view of the park entrance.

Pleasantview on Willowdale Avenue, Lake Mascuppic, in the mid-1950s.

The bathhouses at Pleasantview on Willowdale Avenue directly across the lake from the ballroom. This is all empty beachfront today, with no evidence of such activity in the past.

A view across the lake from Pleasantview, looking toward the old ballroom.

A close-up of the old ballroom and restaurant owned by the Boston and Northern Street Railway Company. It burned in the late 1920s.

The new ballroom. The piers of the old ballroom can be seen next to the new one, built in 1928 by Harry Kittridge. The Lakeview ballroom was Dracut's most famous site. The dance floor measured 12,000 square feet, with an open balcony on the lake side. It was modeled after the Mormon Temple in Salt Lake City, Utah.

A postcard view of the ballroom's interior.

Amusement rides. The roller coaster was constructed in front of and on both sides of Kittredge's Ballroom, *c.* 1929.

66

Willow Dale Chips packaging. This image was taken from an old potato chip box in the collection of the Dracut Historical Society.

The store at the trolley turnaround at Lakeview. It was run by Gertrude Young in the 1920s.

The Kinghorn children of Dracut. The youngsters pose outside the tearoom attached to the ballroom, which was also managed by their grandmother, Gertrude Young.

Tyngsborough Road looking toward Stewart Street in a 1940s postcard.

Ricky Keefe in the ice at Beaver Brook, c. 1930. His grandson, the author, did not inherit this ability.

Ricky and a few disciples at Beaver Brook in more moderate weather, c. 1930. No swimmers have come to this beach in over forty years.

A group of Dracut citizens enjoying the flooding of Beaver Brook from the Parker Avenue Bridge, Saturday, November 5, 1927. The underpinnings of this bridge were hit by a truck in 1957, and it fell into the brook.

The first Eastern Massachusetts bus on the Lakeview Avenue route. The operator is Frank Bancroft. The first St. Theresa's Church is in the background of the photograph.

An anniversary celebration. Allen Seamens and Jack Keefe pull the old fire wagon up Lakeview Avenue on the 250th anniversary of the founding of the town in 1951.

The predecessor to the bus in the opposite picture, 1931. This open car traveled daily between Lowell and Lakeview. The fare was 5¢.

The hill on Pleasant Street rising to Hovey Square. Many changes have occurred since this Civil War-period landscape was photographed on a height from Swain Street. The Hillside Church in this photograph, built in 1834, burned and was rebuilt. The second church was torn

down in the late 1960s. The building in the center, on Peppermint, formerly Tanhouse Brook, was perhaps the hat factory that replaced the tannery that was probably the original building on the site.

A quiet Lakeview Avenue in the 1920s. New Boston Road veers to the right. Today, the scene would include a travel agency, hairdresser, and Dracut High School.

Accident! A bakery truck (note the loaves of bread) collides with a highway department truck at the Lotus Filling Station (later Polly's Variety), at the corner of Mammoth Road and Lakeview Avenue. The license plate reads 1937.

On Pleasant Street. Gregory Panagiotakos and his sister Cleo parked outside the Enoch, or Timothy Frye house on Pleasant Street about 1950. The house was torn down in the 1970s. It faced Swain Street.

Curiosity. A crowd gathers to assess the damage.

A winter scene at the corners of Hildreth Street and Colburn Avenue, 1930s.

A toast. Glasses are raised in a toast at Mountain View Baseball Park at Lakeview, *c.* 1890.

Four

Work

The wagon from the Wiggin Farm, Mammoth Road. John C. Wiggin was a grocer who lived and worked at his brother Charles' farm on Mammoth Road, near Nashua Road. Two other brothers, Parker and Frederich, also lived here. They were carpenters about 1895. The house was razed in the late 1970s. Condominiums are now on the site.

Elizah Axon, *c.* 1900. Axon lived on 7th Avenue in Lowell, but for several years around the turn of the century he was the rural free delivery postman for Dracut, Collinsville, and Willowdale.

Mr. and Mrs. Emery Gauren, behind the counter of their variety and grocery store at the corner of Hemlock and Merrimac Avenue. Mrs. Hamel and her son are being served in this postcard photograph, *c.* 1922.

Armistice Day, November 11, 1918, at the Merrimac Woolen Mill on Pleasant Street at the Navy Yard. The tall chimney is part of the building where gas was manufactured to light the mill. The house in the center right was the residence of Humbert Thomas. The building in the right foreground is the house of the Bachman Hose fire company, built in 1883.

The Navy Yard was a deep valley before the last glacier receded about thirty thousand years ago. When the ice retreated, it deposited an enormous amount of sand in the depression. When the foundations for the mill in this photograph were laid in 1862, it was necessary to drive piles very deep into the ground to find bedrock. The pre-glacial surface is over 30 feet deep here.

Polly's Variety. The proprietor of Polly's Variety (formerly the Lotus Filling Station on the corner of Mammoth Road and Lakeview Avenue—see bottom of p.74), Polly Urquhardt is as famous a personage as any who lived in Dracut between the 1940s and the 1980s. She delivered

newspapers by bicycle and wagon well into her eighties, she pumped gas, and never allowed smoking in the store she ran singlehandedly.

Polly's Variety, summertime in the 1940s.

Polly herself, across the street from her store, in a new fur coat. She cradles an animal which has been identified as either a dog, cat, or fox.

Michael Collins. Mr. Collins purchased the area which now includes the Collinsville Mills on March 31, 1880. Waterpower had been used to fuel a gristmill and a sawmill from 1753 to 1773 by Joseph Hamblett. It was purchased by the Wilson brothers—Life, David, Cyrus, and Charles—and was known as Wilson's Mills until well into the late 1800s. Collins built the existing mills in 1886. He also built the mill houses, some of which remain on Mill Street. His residence was close at hand on the corner of Mill Street and on Lakeview Avenue. New machinery was installed, stores were opened, and the government established a post office and appointed Mr. Collins postmaster.

Michael Collins in front of the mill he constructed in Collinsville, *c.* 1900. Collins is wearing the derby hat, and with him is Bartholomew J. Cullinan, assistant superintendent.

John J. Kiernan and Son, Grocers, Lakeview Avenue. This is a relatively recent (1950s) photograph of Dracut's first post office, which has seen many changes.

The weave room at the Collinsville Mills, later called the Beaver Brook Mills, *c.* 1905.

A copy of the official photograph from the main office of the Beaver Brook Mills, *c.* 1900. Lakeview Avenue is still unpaved.

Operations at the Beaver Brook Mills, June 9, 1902. At its peak, under Michael Collins' superintendency, the mill employed about 260 operatives and produced about 230,000 yards of cloth. Collins sold the mill to the American Woolen Company in 1899. His original wooden three-story building was destroyed by fire. The American Woolen Company built the existing brick structure which became known as the Beaver Brook Mills.

Bringing in the bales at Beaver Brook,
c. 1910.

The exhibit of the Merrimac Woolen
Mills, at the Navy Yard on Pleasant Street
in Dracut, on display at the Colombian
Exposition World's Fair, Chicago, 1892. The
first plaid materials and shawls woven in this
country were displayed and are shown in the
upper center of the picture. The exhibit won
a gold medal.

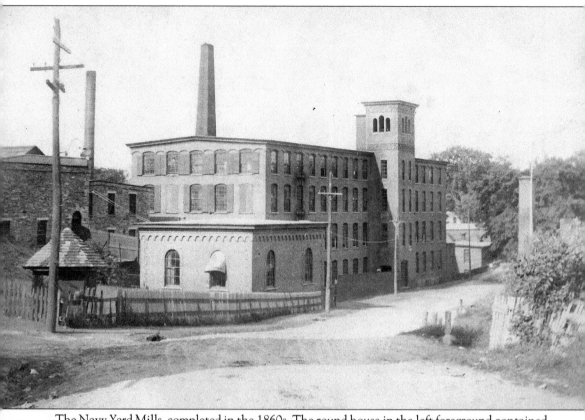

The Navy Yard Mills, completed in the 1860s. The round house in the left foreground contained four hydrants. The stone building on the extreme left, which is still intact, was used for cloth inspection and shipping.

The first mill recorded on this site was built by Ephraim Hildreth and Ebenezer Goodhue about 1739. In 1762 it was sold to Ezekial Hale along with a dwelling house and blacksmith's shop. Hale's original house was on the north side of Pleasant Street and was removed to accommodate the electric cars. It is now 1092 Lakeview Avenue. During the latter years of the eighteenth century and for most of the nineteenth, many changes took place at this site. Mills of all types functioned here: corn, fulling, grist, saw, cotton, and then woolen mills. The histories of some are well recorded; many, however, are only mentioned vaguely in the annals of history.

Dye House crew, Navy Yard Mills, *c.* 1893.

Workmen at the construction site of the
Lakeview Ballroom, early 1920s.

A clean-up crew. Women volunteers clean the Hillside Church, *c.* 1926. From left to right are: (front row) Mrs. Robert Derbyshire, Mrs. John Smith, Mrs. Ethel Drendel, and Mrs. Flora Shanks; (second row) Mrs. Annie Coburn, Miss Irene Hill, Mrs. Henry Hamer, and Mrs. Ralph Giffin; (back row) Sarah Nichols, Mrs. Herbert Lyon, Mrs. Roy Laurie, and Mrs. William Giffen. Roger William Giffen is in the background.

The Lowell and Dracut Street Railway in the early 1880s. The car barn in the background was at the Navy Yard corner of Lakeview and Pleasant Street at the present mini-mall site.

Lakeview Park employees at the annual outing, *c.* 1923. The outing was held at the Mountain Rock picnic area at the opposite end of Lake Mascuppic from Lakeview Park.

On the farm. Zoel Houle poses with his hens on the Arlington Street farm, 1920s. Mr. Houle produced the first commercial cement blocks in Dracut.

Making change. George Grondine makes change at his filling station on Nashua Road, mid-1950s. The station, across from Alexander's pharmacy, is still in operation.

A group of Dracut dignitaries, assembled at the Moses Greeley Parker Library in 1950. The group had just returned from Boston, where Warren W. Fox gave a dinner and theater party for town officials with whom he had served prior to his retirement. The group gave him the camera with which the picture was taken. Seated in front, from left to right, are John Brox, William Bromley, Edward Dockett, Moses Daigle, Walter Garland, and Norman Peavey. Those identified in the back row include Warren Fox, Walter Wagner, Percy Center, Sam Pillsbury, John Callahan, Conant Udell, Hector Berube, Amadee Guimond, Daniel Hanson, James Taylor, and Valmore Cornellier.

Home on leave, 1944. Chief Petty Officer Jack Keefe poses with his brothers Ray and Tommy (foreground) and his sister Anna, in front of the family home at 188 Pleasant Street. Jack's ship, the USS *Roberts*, a destroyer, led the attack and was sunk in the Battle of Leyte Gulf later that year. Jack was Dracut's postmaster in later years. Ray was a fireman and Tommy is presently a town assessor.

George Kelley and his Devon oxen at his Arlington Street farm. After returning from the California Gold Rush, Kelley settled on the family farm. He used these oxen to haul stone from Loon Hill in order to build the enormous walls which are still visible at the old farm site near Kelley Road.

Another photograph of the store on the corner of Pleasant and Sladen Street which was taken well before the beginning of this century. It served as the community package store from the late 1920s until fairly recently.

The Keefes. Ricky and Marietta Keefe dance the Cakewalk in costumes imported from Ireland, Fourth of July, early 1930s. He was an Eastern Massachusetts bus driver, a dealer in war surplus, and a champion swimmer. He and his wife were also semi-professional dancers. They lived at 188 Pleasant Street.

Dracut High School cheerleaders. Ricky and Marietta Keefe's granddaughter, also Marietta, is the fourth from the right in this 1953 photograph. She is now the wife of Brigadier General Richard Aldrich (retired).

Dracut Center Grammar School, 1892–93. Miss Julia Bixby is the teacher.

Kenwood School, undated. There appear to be only forty-five stars on the flag.

Primary class at the Navy Yard School, 28 Pleasant Street. This school preceded the Parker Avenue School. No date is given for this photograph, but the school burned down in the 1870s.

The Dracut Graded School, held in the same location where the town offices are today, late 1880s.

The Willet Farm. Pictured, from left to right, are Ruby, Carrie, Helen, Vivian, Maude, and Mrs. Thomas B. (Harriet) Willet. The farm was on Mammoth Road near Nashua Road in 1902.

Mr. and Mrs. Emery (Albine) Gaurin and mother-in-law Mrs. Latour. The Gaurins ran a grocery store in the late 1930s on Merrimac Avenue. They are behind the counter in an earlier photograph on p.78.

Seventh or eighth grade Parker Avenue class photograph, 1926. From left to right are: (seated) unknown, Adeline Silva, Irene Mitchell, unknown, Marguerite ?, Roland Morrison, Anna Keefe, Euginia Caragianas, Alice Conlon, Stella Dumont, and Charlotte Cheneval; (standing) Al Merrill, Freddy ?, Edward Goodhue, George Neofotistos, Gus Wagner, Douglas Blizzard, Mrs. Spalding (principal), John Neofotistos, Tom Grogan, J. Hudzik, Nick Sperounis, and Alton Garland.

Gold Star Mothers at the dedication of the Honor Roll in Collinsville, November 14, 1943. The Gold Star Mothers are Mrs. Harriet Morse and Mrs. Agnes Tymula. The soldier is Mr. Dys, and the sailor is William Collins.

100

ADMINISTRATOR'S SALE.

TO BE SOLD
AT PUBLIC AUCTION,

On Wednesday the 30th day of April, at the House of the late ENOCH FRYE, in Dracutt, One pair of Young Oxen, one pair of two-year old Steers, 3 Cows, 1 horse, 2 two-year old Heifers, 1 Swine, 1 Ox Wagon, 1 Horse Wagon, 1 old Chaise, 1 pair of old Chiase Wheels, 1 six Ox Plough, 1 Horse Plough, 1 set of plough Irons, 2 Iron Bars, 3 ——— 20 bushels of Corn, 8 bushels of Rye, 30 bushels of Potatoes,--a small lot of Timber, some split Stone, some Cider and Casks, and various other aricles too numerous to mention. ☞Sale to commence at one o'clock, P. M.   Conditions made known at time of sale.

LIFE HAMBLET, Adm'r.

Dracutt, April 14, 1834.

Sale of goods belonging to the late Enoch Frye. Mr. Frye lived at the house on Pleasant Street facing Swain Street. His father fought in the Revolutionary War before he was in his teens. Enoch died in 1834. This poster announced the sale of his earthly goods.

The original St. Theresa's Church, built in 1927 on Lakeview Avenue.

A disastrous fire. St. Theresa's Church (see p. 27) is shown here burning to the ground on January 1938. The rebuilding of the church was eased by fate. A shipment of bricks ordered by the Lowell Textile School was found to be unsuitable. It was sold to the parish very reasonably. Note the similarity of the brick in the church with that of the early buildings of UMass Lowell, North Campus.

The Marquis de Marisquelles. No history of Dracut could be complete without a depiction of the Marquis Marie-Louis Amant Ansart de Marisquelles. He was born in France in 1752. At military academy he became expert in casting cannon. At the outbreak of American rebellion in 1776, Ansart offered his services to America. He was appointed inspector general of foundries and colonel of artillery. Paul Revere studied under his tutelage. On active duty, as aide-de-camp to General Sullivan, he was wounded. He settled in Dracut in 1781 with his wife, Catherine Wimble, and had twelve children. He attempted to raise silkworms he bought from France after that country's rebellion, but failed. He is buried in the Oakland Cemetery, now in Lowell. His house stands at 510 Varnum Avenue in Lowell. Lafayette came to visit him after the war. He is one of the unsung heroes of the Revolutionary War.

The Little Farm. Jim Patterson leads the cows out onto the road from the farm of Charles Little at 1660 Lakeview Avenue. Jim lived at number 1056, c. 1920. The Little Farm was directly across from the junior high school and the historical society. The farm was on both sides of the street and had 110 cattle and 500 hogs.

In the 1950s the land was developed and a housing estate named Rainbow Acres was quickly filled by city dwellers anxious for the peace and expansiveness of the suburbs. Dracut had begun to grow smaller, however. When the town was first laid out, it consisted of 22,334 acres. By 1914, it had been reduced to 12,530.

An aerial view of the Shaw Farm on New Boston Road. The farm, still very much in operation, was established in 1908.

Beaver Brook Farm on Mammoth Road, now the Justin Richardson Farm. This picture is taken from an advertising ink blotter made in 1928. The farm is still in operation.

Captain Sydney Stuart, USN, born June 4, 1857, at Erie, Pennsylvania. After a short stay in Norwich, VT, his family settled in Dracut. He graduated from West Point in 1880, third in his class. In 1884, at age twenty-seven, he was appointed assistant professor of natural and experimental philosophy at the military academy. He devised a formula for smokeless powder and was working on his discovery when he was fatally injured in a gun cotton explosion on April 29, 1899. He was buried at West Point at sunset on May 3, 1899, with full military honors.

Belle Stuart. A small article in the *Lowell Sun*, December 26, 1899, reads, "Miss Belle Stuart, formerly of Dracut, has resigned as principal of the training school at New Bedford. She will go to Washington, DC to care for the children of her brother Captain Sydney Stuart who was killed last year in a powder explosion."

The charred remains of Michael Collins' woolen mill at Beaver Brook at Collinsville. The mill burned April 18, 1899. The new mill is in the background. The house on the right was at one time Michael Collins' residence. At the time of the fire it was a mill boarding house run by Mrs. Silk. It was moved in two parts to Primrose Hill Road and remains two separate buildings.

A postcard view of the falls at Beaver Brook.

A photograph of the 100th anniversary of the building of the Old Yellow Meeting House, taken

in 1894. The belfry was added in 1869 and the bell was installed in 1884.

Miss Nikki Pappas at her home at 230 Dracut Street, just over the line from Lowell. Miss Pappas married Reverend John Sarantos of Lowell. The couple still resides there.

The Pappas family. In this 1925 photograph of the Pappas family are, from left to right, Vasil J. Pappas, Helen J. Pappas (holding her son Leonides), and Mary Socorelis. Helen (Socorelis) Pappas was born in Langodia, Greece, in 1893 and came to the United States in 1900 at age seven. When her father collected her at Ellis Island, she handed him back the $40 fare he had paid for her passage, which she earned by singing for the passengers during her thirty-six day journey across the Atlantic. At fourteen, she would buy fruit wholesale at the Vlahos Fruit Company in Lowell and, by herself, drive a horse and wagon from Market Street to Chelmsford, Forge Village, Littleton, Westford, and Groton. She was a well-known singer of Greek folk songs and recorded several of them.

Select School.

J. S. PHILLIPS

Will open a SELECT SCHOOL at the VESTRY of the CENTRE MEETINGHOUSE, in Dracut, on

MONDAY, MARCH 12th, INST.

To continue eleven weeks.

TUITION---$4.50 per scholar, for the common English Branches. One Dollar extra for each of the Languages, or for Higher Mathematics.

For further particulars inquire of Geo. W. Coburn, Chas. B. Varnum, or J. C. Kimball.

Dracut, Mass., March 2d, 1860.

A Dracut lyceum. Regarding this notice, Silas Coburn, in his *History of Dracut* (1922) writes, "A lyceum was organized at the Center about 1855. It is said to have been very successful, but no records have been found."

One of the fruitful fields of the Beaver Brook Farm, 1917. This piece of land faces Water Street.

St. Mary's Holy Name Society. This banquet commemorated the 50th anniversary of the founding of St. Mary's Holy Name Society, November 7, 1954.

The Parker Tavern on Broadway, erected as a dwelling in 1764 by Josiah Wood. By 1807, the building was a popular tavern and eventually became a stop on the Underground Railroad to Canada. It was torn down in 1965. The entire second floor was a dance hall. During the Colonial period, this tavern was very well known throughout New England for its warm society and great elegance. People from Chelmsford, Dunstable, and further flung communities would sleigh in to dance "with supper provided." It was well attended by the founders and early citizenry of Lowell.

Doorway, Parker Tavern, 1905. The elaborate Georgian entrance to the Parker Tavern rivaled those of much larger and wealthier communities like Salem and Newburyport in their heydays.

Nowhere in Dracut. Printed in golden ink on the upper left of this yellowed postcard are the words,"Greetings from Dracut, Mass." It was mailed on November 22, 1909. The scene is nowhere in Dracut.

A mill on Victory Lane on Beaver Brook, north of the Parker Avenue Bridge. Paper was made here as early as 1839. From about 1883, it was operated by Morton L. Bassett and Company under the name Beaver Brook Paper Mill. This building burned on July 4, 1911.

Inside the image: "BETTER TIMES" AUSPICES OF PARENT-TEACHER ASSOCIATION COLLINSVILLE MASS NOV. 17-18, 1932

PHOTO BY GENERAL 2 YELLS W MEDFORD

Better times. The title of the 1932 Collinsville Parent-Teacher Association variety show exemplifies post-Depression attitudes across the entire country.

A precarious pose. The lady is unidentified, but the bridge is the old Parker Avenue Bridge, which sank into the brook in 1957 when a truck struck its underpinnings.

Bridge over Richardson Brook. This bridge spanned Richardson Brook in Kenwood just before it runs into the Merrimac.

Costas Caragianas. The caption on this *Lowell Sun* photograph reads, "Grizzled combat veteran Costas L. Caragianas of Dracut yesterday was promoted to the rank of Brigadier General, it was announced by the White House." During World War II he served with General Patton and won a Silver Star, three Bronze Stars, a presidential citation, and a medal from the French. General Caragianas resides at Pleasant Street in Dracut. His is the earliest Greek family to arrive in Dracut.

Broadway School, first grade class, 1937. This was the last class to graduate (three years later in grade four) from this school. In the front row, from left to right, are Helen Saja, Josephine Schiripo, Therese Guillemette, Margaret Schiripo, Rita Snowpaskis, Pearl Richardson, Tolly Kerepka, Imogine Foy, Elvina Leczynski, Mary Cieslik, and Charlotte Pelczar. The back row is composed of Allen Richardson and Roscoe Richardson. Included in the middle row are Gilbert Richardson, Edie Levesque, Gardner Richardson, Frank Sandelli, and Victor Guillemette.

Brigadier General Philip Reade, born in Dracut in 1844. He was the author of a genealogy of the Hildreth family from which he is descended and contributed to Silas Colburn's *History of Dracut* (1922). He served as a secret agent during the Civil War and later was awarded the Congressional Medal of Honor for action during the Spanish-American War in which he served both in Cuba and the Philippines. He also supervised the construction of the final 1,500 miles of telegraph service across the United States from Santa Fe to San Diego. This epic adventure, filled with peril from the natives and Mexicans, as well as the terrain and nature, is recorded in his detailed journals.

Reade's secret mission. This note reads: "April 7th, 1864. To all Officers of the U.S. Army or Navy or U.S. Volunteers, the bearer, Philip Reade, is on Secret Service, Union Service, and is acting under orders from me, and is engaged in gathering information about the enemy. [signed] Benj. F. Butler, Maj. Genl. Comdg."

Wendell Corey, Dracut native. Mr. Corey and Barbara Stanwyck are menaced in *Thelma Jordon*, 1949. This is a film noir classic in which a district attorney (Corey) becomes involved with a murder suspect (Stanwyck). Corey was born at Hovey Square, where his parents had a grocery store at 456 Hovey Avenue.

Carbine Williams. In this film, Wendell Corey played the sympathetic warden to Jimmy Stewart's title role.

Speedway program. The Dracut Speedway flourished in the 1940s, but was quickly closed in the early fifties soon after an out-of-control car crashed into the stands, killing one of the spectators.

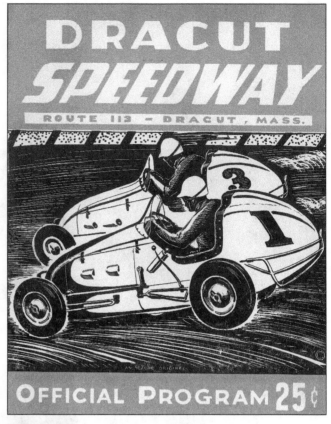

Daredevils. "Frisky's Hollywood Hell Drivers, Men Who Defy Death" were among the contenders at the Dracut Speedway. The track was located on Broadway where it meets Arlington Street in the 1940s.

A view of the track at the speedway from the stands, 1940.

Dracut High School faculty, 1935. From left to right are: (front row) Arthur Skandalis, Donald Shanahan, James Riley (principal), Marie (Condon) McKenna, Ora (McLaughlin) Parks, and Katherine (Boland) Prior; (back row) Henry Koneiczny, John Guenard, Coach Spencer Sullivan, Rene Bernardin, Pauline Varnum, Helen Shea, and Jeanne Dozois.

Captain Gilbert Coburn's sawmill on Bridge Street opposite Jericho Road, built in 1840. The Captain's grandfather Edward, a soldier during the French and Indian War, was born in Dracut in 1721. In 1769, he bought land a few rods north of the state line. This photograph predates 1863, when the farm was sold.

Troop #38's float in the 250th Anniversary Parade, 1951.

Third degree team, Dracut Grange, Fall 1906. In the front row, from left to right, are Mrs. John Weinbeck, Mrs. Mabel Colburn, Mrs. George Fox, Mrs. Norman Peavey, Mrs. Vivia Fox, Mrs Chester Colburn, and Mrs. Eva Blanchard. In the middle row, from left to right, are Mrs. Jesse Currier, Mrs. Asa Stickney, Mrs. Loretta McManmon, Mrs. Westcott, Mrs. Hodges, and Mrs. Welts. Included in the back row are Mrs. Otley, Miss Mildred Vinal, Miss Helen Fox, Mrs. Lillian Parker, and Miss Mary Hilton.

Overseas communication. *The Navy Yard News* was produced by the Navy Yard Mills during the World War II years to keep in contact with employees who were away on active service.

Navy Yard News excerpt. Page eighteen of *The Navy Yard News* reads, "These are only a few of our blanket room cuties." From left to right are: Rutha Lynch, Dot Lynch, Mabel Sheehan, Millie Sheehan, and Frankie Riordan.

The first graduating class from Dracut High School. These are the members of the Class of 1936.

Dracut plays Chelmsford, 1946. This Dracut team, coached by newcomer Ed Murphy, was undefeated this year.

A presidential greeting. Brigadier General James F. McManmon is greeted by Franklin D. Roosevelt, *c.* 1943. McManmon was an All-American Guard at Princeton in 1922. He successfully went in search of oil in the Oklahoma fields and also became involved in banking in New York and Tulsa. During World War II he was assistant chief of staff under General Hap Arnold and headed an Allied mission to China. He remained after the war as an advisor to Chiang Kai-Shek. He was vice president of the World Commerce Corporation, Massachusetts Airport commissioner, and held several other significant positions in business and government. FDR detoured through Dracut on a tour especially to renew acquaintances with the general.

Two citizens of Dracut at the crossroads, *c.* 1917.

Acknowledgments

Many people contributed time and effort as well as their photographs to this endeavor. Rick Harvey of the Media Center at UMass Lowell copied several of the photographs used in the book. Esther Garland of the Dracut Historical Society was full of information and good advice. Harvey Gagnon, Norma Taplin, Bud Paquin, and Jim Kiernan (also of the Dracut Historical Society) were very supportive to the effort. These are some of the unsung present-day heroes in a long line who have been most instrumental in keeping Dracut's past intact. There are few communities that have a society as active and generous with their time and effort as Dracut's. Donat Paquet should be commended for his tireless efforts to record Dracut. Much of Dracut's treasured past remains intact; valuable papers, artifacts, books, photographs, etc. are secure under the protective wings of these people. Paul Dumont allowed me to pick through his extraordinary postcard and photograph collection. The great shots of Polly's Variety are his. Tom and Jimmy Keefe of Keefe's Antiques, Dracut's oldest extant antique business, came forward with gems from their collection acquired through three generations of collectors. My brother Pat also had a few pictures to offer. My own collection is represented, started when I was about ten with faded daguerreotypes rescued from my grandfather's attic on the corner of Swain and Pleasant Streets; so is a 1906 postcard found fairly recently in a flea market in Trois Riviere, Quebec, sent back to *Memere* from an emigrant granddaughter in Collinsville in 1905. Kathleen and Philip Hammar of Nashua, NH, have given me photographs as have Reverend John and Niki Sarantos of Lowell, MA. Donald Kinghorn put a few in the post to me. There are several other people who have offered sage suggestions and helped to point me in useful directions. Charlotte Pincense allowed me to take her "Tony's" photograph from the wall at Debbie's. Charles Panagiotakos lent me photographs of his Dracut cousins and pulled a Wendell Covey photograph out of the air.

My daughter Cait typed all the text from my erratic scrawls onto a disc for revision and did a considerable amount of editing. Maire, my wife, has remained remarkably civil throughout the project. Several of life's pleasures have been put aside for forages at the historical society, and innumerable phone calls have been answered on my behalf. I have even browbeaten some of my students, both present and past, into the search for old photographs. My thanks to all.